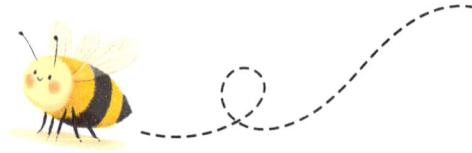

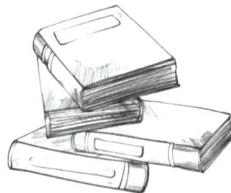

LESSONS
from
NATURE

Bees don't have tentacles

Flamingos don't have antlers.

Giraffes don't have webbed feet.

Octopuses don't have feathers.

Bunnies don't have narwhal horns

Monkeys don't have fish tails.

Pigs don't have trunks.

Elephants don't have snouts.

Boys don't have vaginas.

Girls don't have penises.

The End.

www.ingramcontent.com/pod-product-compliance
Lightning Source LLC
Chambersburg PA
CBHW040811300326
41914CB00065B/1491

www.ingramcontent.com/pod-product-compliance
Lightning Source LLC
Chambersburg PA
CBHW040811300326
41914CB00065B/1491